Double Wedding Ring Patchwork

Ingeborg Kooijman

Kangaroo Press

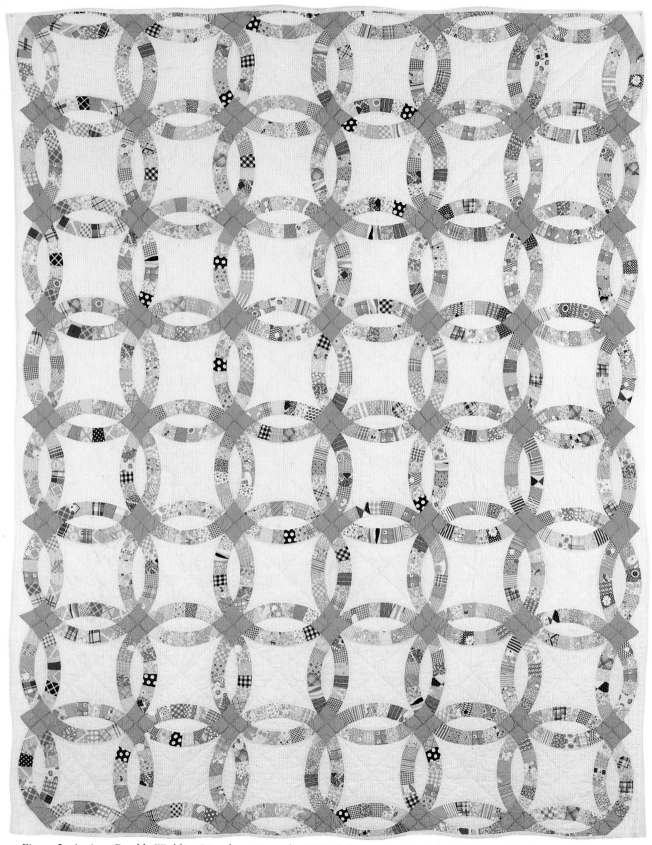

Figure 2 *Antique Double Wedding Ring from Kentucky, 1920, belonging to Marie-José Schwarts-Rottier,*
180 cm x 225 cm (71" x 88½")

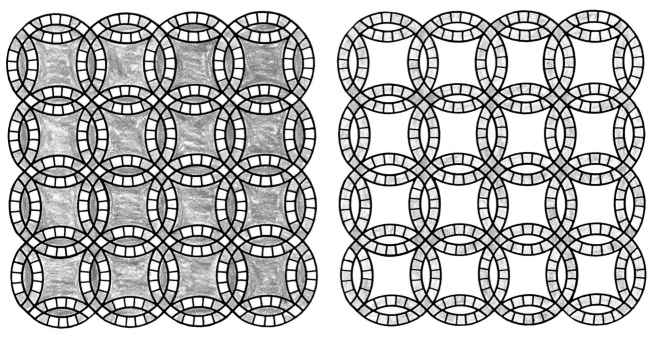

Figure 3a, 3b *Variations of figure 3*

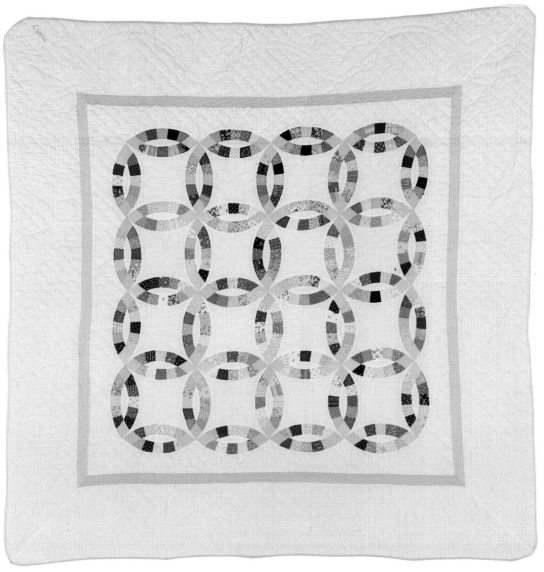

Figure 3 *Maryvonne Fontaine, 150 cm x 140 cm (59" x 55")*

3

1 The Double Wedding Ring

In the nineteenth century in America it was traditional to give a wedding quilt as a gift to a young bride. Often this would be a very beautiful appliqué quilt, decorated with flowers and hearts. At the beginning of this century a new pattern began to appear: the Double Wedding Ring. This wedding quilt was very popular in the Depression of the 1930s as the pattern used up small pieces of fabric in a very practical way.

The quilt symbolised joy and romance in a period when life was particularly drab. It was an accomplishment to make a beautiful quilt from small left-over scraps of fabric. The back of the quilt was usually made from cotton flour sacks.

The pattern of the Double Wedding Rings was probably introduced by the German immigrants who came to Pennsylvania in the seventeenth century. The block was originally derived from a wedding ring that was very popular in Germany in the fifteenth and sixteenth centuries, the Gimmal ring. This consisted of two rings which could be twisted around each other. During the engagement period the man and the woman would wear a ring each. In the wedding ceremony the rings were twisted together and then worn by the woman.

Another Gimmal ring has three parts. The two outside rings form two hands and the middle ring has an inscription which is only visible when both the outside rings are removed.

The popularity of this pattern and its many variations led to its becoming known in different states of America by many other names, including: Circle Upon Circle, Double Wedding Bands, The Endless Chain, Golden Wedding Ring, Here Comes the Bride, Indian Wedding Ring, King Tut, Lover's Knot, Patriot's Pride, Pickle Dish, Rainbow Wedding Ring, Rings Around the World, When Circles Get Together, Wedding Ring Chain.

The Double Wedding Ring is not one of the easiest blocks, but by following the pattern very carefully even an inexperienced quilter can get very good results.

List of Requirements
- graph paper
- sharp pencils (HB)
- paper and fabric scissors or rotary cutter
- ruler, triangle and compass
- cardboard (medium thickness) or pattern paper
- fine sandpaper
- glue
- pins, needles, cotton (preferably 100% cotton)
- quilting cotton, quilting needles
- cotton fabric (preferably 100% cotton)
- Vilene No. 180
- wadding or fibrefill

2 Different Shapes

Each of the variety of Double Wedding Ring patterns has its own characteristics and focal point.

Overall Double Wedding Ring patterns can be divided into square types (figures 1, 5, 82) and circular types (figures 4, 7, 85, 86). Both types can be worked straight or diagonally. With a straight DWR (Double Wedding Ring) the rings are placed in a square (figure 9) and with a diagonal DWR the rings are placed in a diamond shape (figure 8). The differences become most noticeable when looking at the central piece. The quilt by Maryvonne Fontaine on page 3 is a good example of a straight round DWR; the quilt on page 22 is a round DWR made in a diamond shape.

The points where the rings cross over each other can be square (figure 10 and the quilt on page 19) or pointed shapes (figure 11 and the quilt on page 11). The crossover points can be made in one colour (see the quilt by Corrie Hagendijk on page 18) or in two colours, as in the quilt by Karin Jongeleen on page 30.

The rings can also be made in continuous colours over the cross-over points (see quilt by Ingeborg Kooijmans on page 15).

The central piece can be made to continue into the corner points, as in the quilt shown on pages 26 and 27, or be made with square or diamond shaped points (figures 12 and 13).

The thickness of the rings is usually one-eighth of the diameter of the circle. If the DWR has a diameter of 32 cm (12") then the rings and crossover points will be 4 cm (1½") wide.

You can of course experiment with the sizes, as some fabrics might work better with wider or narrower rings. The rings can be made up out of one piece of fabric (see quilt by Ingeborg Kooijman on page 31) or divided into equal pieces (figures 14 and 15) or unequal pieces (figure 16). If you have chosen even-sized large pieces you can divide the rings into an even number (figure 14) or an uneven number of same-sized pieces (figure 15). The rings in the quilt by Karin Jongeleen on page 30 are divided into six equal pieces, while the rings in the quilt by Pauline van Giessen (on the front cover) are divided into five equal pieces. If you are working

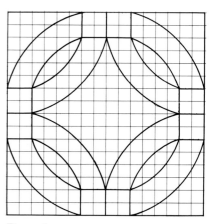

Figure 4

Figure 5

Figure 6

Figure 7

Figure 8

Figure 9

Figure 10

Figure 11

Figure 12

Figure 13

Figure 14

Figure 15

Figure 16

with an uneven number of pieces the centre piece can be kept in the same colour. You may wish to use a certain piece of fabric for your quilt, when the size of the fabric can determine the size of the rings.

The arches and arched diamond shapes together form the background of the DWR. These can be made all in one colour, or you could choose to use one colour for the arches and another for the diamond shape, as in the quilt by Joke Nieboer on page 19.

With a light coloured plain background fabric the DWR will give a very restful effect. Do not use a pure white fabric, as this can give the quilt a harsh and impersonal appearance. An off-white or broken white or ecru colour will give a warmer effect. Instead of plain it is also possible to use a neutral patterned fabric, as in the quilt by Clara Janssens on page 11. Such fabrics at a distance give a plain effect. In general patterned background fabrics come across with a warmer effect than plain fabrics of the same colour. When you use neutral patterned fabrics for a background quilting work can be kept to a minimum, while making the quilt in a plain fabric will require more quilting. If your choice of background fabric is too busily patterned the rings can tend to disappear into the background, although in my own traditional DWR (page 15) I have chosen a busy fabric on purpose. Here the outside rings more or less disappear into the background. You can also keep changing the background fabric.

Who will be using the quilt?
If you are making the quilt for your own use the choice of colours will ba a lot easier than if you were making it as a wedding gift for a friend or relative, especially if you wish to keep it as a surprise. Keep in mind the effect desired.

Do you want to work older or used fabrics into the quilt? — for romance and memories to be cherished by the person getting married. It is also a good idea to use scraps of fabric from relatives and friends in such a quilt. Using left-over scraps of fabric will give you a 'scrap' quilt which will need to have a plain background.

If you are using older pieces of fabric you will need to realise they may well vary in quality and thickness. As far as possible try to use fabrics of

Figure 17 *Lia Heuvelman, 100 cm x 130 cm (39¹/₂" x 51")*

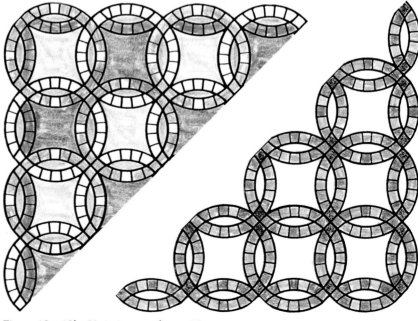

Figure 18a, 18b *Variations on figure 18*

6

similar thickness; if necessary, iron thin or stretch fabrics onto a piece of thin Vilene.

This method can also be used when you are working with silk fabrics. Do remember that silk is a very easily damaged, quick to tear and difficult to work fabric. A silk quilt is therefore less suitable for use as a bed quilt.

There are some other points to consider when making a quilt as a gift. Will it need to be a bed quilt or a wallhanging? Is the decor of the house modern or classic? The quilt should blend in with the interior decoration. In a modern decor striped fabrics may blend better than fabrics with a small floral pattern. In a modern quilt, for example, the rings could be worked in plain fabric, while the background could be patterned. There are many beautiful fabrics with graphic designs, while some curtain fabrics are especially suitable for quilting (see the quilt by Marijke Snyders on page 31).

An uneven division of the rings will sometimes give a more striking effect than rings divided into equal parts.

The graphic use of colour can also give a modern effect: black, white and grey with a warm colour accent (red or yellow) are an attractive combination.

If your choice is a traditional DWR then fabrics with floral designs, small or large, will achieve the desired effect. A light coloured fabric as background will be more restful and place the emphasis on the rings. Keep in mind, however, that a light coloured fabric will get dirty more easily than a dark one. Quilts can be washed, but after each wash the quality of a quilt deteriorates slightly.

Preparation
Always use a fine, tightly woven fabric. Loose weave fabrics tend to fray, while very thick fabrics tend to bulge in hollow shapes. Cotton fabrics generally make quilting easier.

Always wash the fabric before you use it. By washing is meant placing the fabric in a bucket of warm water for approximately ten minutes. It is not necessary to use soap powder on new

fabric as it should not be dirty. A chemical reaction can be caused by some washing products where traces left in the fabric can contribute to fading.

Quilting fabrics are washed not only to take up shrinkage but also to determine their colourfastness. Red, blue and purple fabrics quite often have a tendency to run. Wash each different coloured piece of fabric separately, then place the wet fabric on an old white towel for approximately fifteen minutes. If the fabric colours the towel, mix two cups of vinegar into a bucket of cold water and leave the fabric in the solution for fifteen minutes. If the colours still run it may be better not to use that fabric.

To make the quilt you can use either cotton or synthetic sewing thread. Remember, however, that synthetic sewing thread will melt if it is ironed at the 'cotton' setting of your iron. It is always safer to use the iron too cool rather than too hot if you are not sure what type of thread has been used.

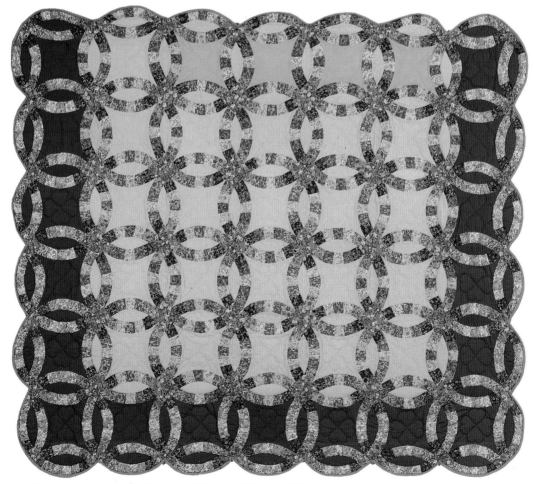

Figure 18 *An van de Giessen, 250 cm x 220 cm (98" x 86½")*

3 Drawing the Double Wedding Ring

Draw the templates for the Double Wedding Ring block onto graph paper with 5 mm divisions. Use a dependable ruler (one with a metal edge is recommended) and a good compass with a sharp pencil. Sharpen the pencil frequently, as wide lines give an unclear image. Always draw one quarter of the pattern (figure 19). A Double Wedding Ring with a diameter of 32 cm (12") will be drawn on a template 16 cm (6") square.

You will need four parts for this pattern:
♦ the middle ('bent diamond' shape)
♦ the corner (square or pointed)
♦ the ellipse
♦ a quarter of the circle (eventually subdivided into an even or uneven number of sections).

Double Wedding Ring with square rings

Example: A Double Wedding Ring with square rings with a diameter of 32 cm (12"). Draw a quarter of the pattern.

Draw a 16 cm (6") square, which is one-quarter of a 32 cm (12") square. Draw a grid inside this, making a 4 cm (1½") square on each corner. This gives the width of the rings and is equal to one-eighth of the diameter of the ring. The 4 cm (1½") squares on each corner should be true to size.

Following figure 20, mark the points A, B, C, D, E, F, G and H in your drawing. Putting the point of the compass on A and the tip of the pencil on C, make a curve from C to F. Leave the point of the compass on A, move the tip of the pencil to B and draw a curve from B to E. Now move the point of the compass to D and the pencil to E and draw a curve from E to B (figure 21). The second ring is made leaving the point of the compass on D and drawing a curve from G to H. This is not strictly necessary, because the ring B, C, F, E is the same as the H, B, E, G ring (figure 21).

The templates for the corner pieces, the ellipse shapes, the ring and

one-quarter of the middle section have now been drawn (figure 22). For the complete middle section you will need to trace the quarter section four times. For accuracy draw this middle section to true size. Draw a 32 cm (12") square divided into sections as shown in figure 23, using AC as the radius for the circular sections.

Dividing the rings

The corner CAF is a right angle (90°). To divide the rings into equal parts you must divide 90° by the number of parts required. If, for example, you want to divide the ellipse shape into five equal parts (as in the quilt on the front cover), the 90° must be divided by 5, which gives 18° (figure 24).

Use a protractor to get the correct angles; the first angle CA1 = 18°; the second angle CA2 = 36°; the third angle CA3 = 54°; the fourth angle CA4 = 72°; the fifth angle CAF = 90°.

You can also choose to divide the rings into uneven pieces, as seen in the quilt by Joke Nieboer on page 19. In this quilt the outside pieces measure 15° (figure 25): CA1 = 15°, IA2 = 60°, FA2 = 15°.

Double Wedding Ring with round rings

A Double Wedding Ring with round rings is made in the same way as a Double Wedding Ring with square rings. First draw one-quarter of the

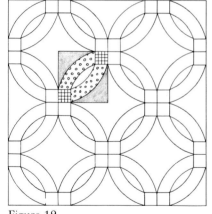

Figure 19

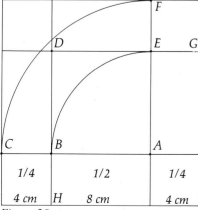

Figure 20

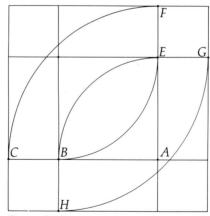

Figure 21

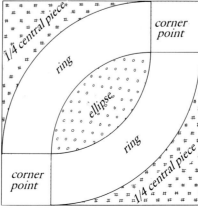

Figure 22

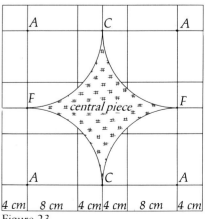

Figure 23

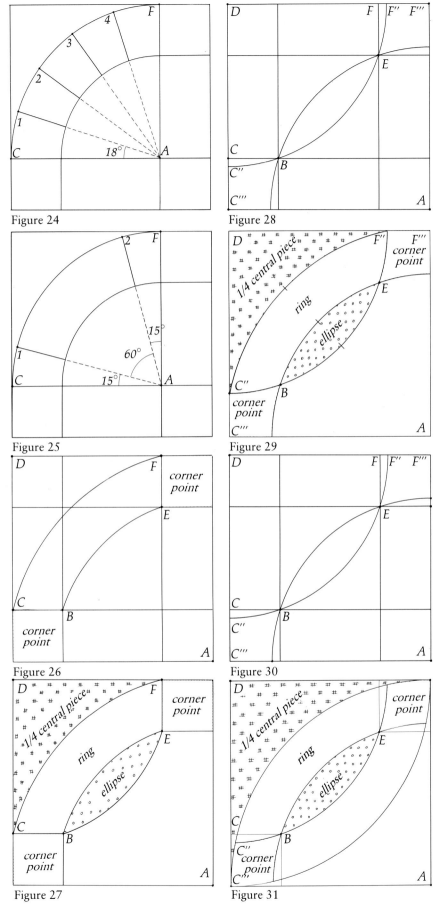

Figure 24

Figure 25

Figure 26

Figure 27

Figure 28

Figure 29

Figure 30

Figure 31

shape; for example, for a circle with a diameter of 32 cm (12") draw a 16 cm (6") square.

Following figure 26, draw a grid in the 16 cm (6") square with 4 cm (1½") squares at the corner points. These give the true size of the corner points. Mark the points A, B, C, D, E and F.

Position the point of the compass on A and the tip of the pencil at C and make a curve from C to F (figure 26). Move the tip of the pencil to B (compass stays on A) and draw a line from B to E.

Now move the compass point to D and with the tip of the pencil on E draw a curve from E to B (figure 27).

Use the method described on the previous page to divide the shape into equal parts.

Round Double Wedding Ring with pointed corner pieces

You can change the corner pieces to pointed shapes, as in the quilt by Clara Janssens on page 11.

Following figure 28, position the compass point on A and the tip of the pencil on E. Draw a curve from E to B and extend it through the points E and B to meet the outside lines of the square. Do the same from point D (figure 28). These lines will form a new point C and a new point F (C", F"). To draw the outside edge of the ring draw a curve from compass point A through C" and F" (figure 29).

The rest of the template is made following the techniques for the square Double Wedding Ring.

Double Wedding Ring with large centre

Another variation on the round Double Wedding Ring is seen in the quilt by Clara Janssens on pages 26 and 27, where the middle section extends right to the corner points.

Using the same grid drawn up in figure 26, draw a curve from compass point A through points B and E, extending it to the outside square (figure 30).

Do the same from point D. Draw a curve from A to the corners marked C''' and F''' to make a larger centre piece (figure 31). Do the same from point D. This gives a clearer corner point.

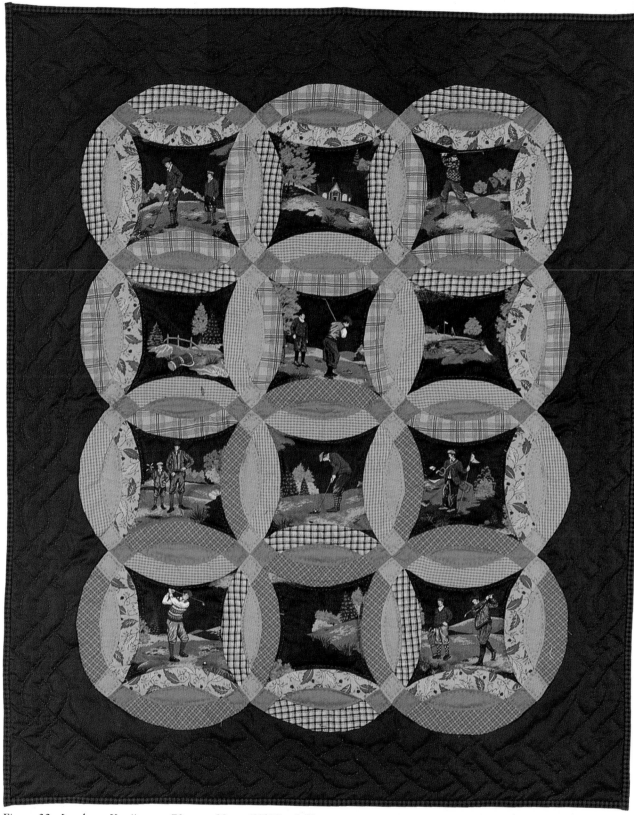

Figure 32 *Ingeborg Kooijmann, 70 cm x 90 cm (27¹/₂" x 36")*

More variations

Variation 1

You can create endless variations. Figure 34 shows a variation on a round Double Wedding Ring with the centre piece extended to the corner points.

To make this block draw a round Double Wedding Ring with the centre extended to the corners (figure 31, page 9). Place a ruler from point A to point B and draw only that part of the line inside the circle. Do the same

Figures 33a, 33b *Variations on figure 33*

Figure 33 *Clara Janssens, 90 cm (36") square*

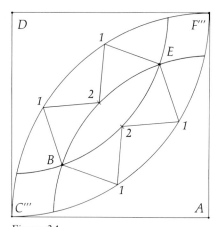

Figure 34

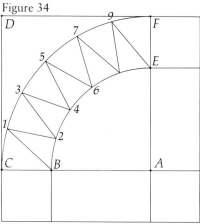

Figure 35

from point A to point E, from point D to point A and from point D to point E. Place the ruler from point D to point A and on the inside of the rings mark the intersecting points. Label the points 1 or 2 as in the figure and connect them together as shown.

Variation 2
Another variation is the Pickle Dish pattern. To draw this start with the grid for the square Double Wedding Ring (figure 22, page 8).

Following figure 35, the inside of the ring is divided equally into five (EAB = 90°; 90° ÷ 5 = 18°). BA2 = 18°; BA4 = 36°, BA6 = 54°, BA8 = 72°. Mark the points of intersection on the inner curve.

The outside of the ring is divided equally into six (FAC = 90°; 90° ÷ 6 = 15°). CA1 = 15°, CA3 = 30°, CA5 = 45°, CA7 = 60°, CA9 = 75°. Mark the points of intersection on the outer curve.

Connect the cutting points together (figure 35). The same method can be used with a round Double Wedding Ring.

Variation 3
This method is a 'quickie', using a sewing machine to achieve a 'scrap' look.

Cut six strips of fabric 114 cm (45") wide. The strips can be all the same depth, or any measurement you choose; however, the six strips together must add up to the radius of the ring, including seam allowances. Sew the six strips together and iron all the seams to one side. Place the pattern on the fabric, making sure the centre of the pattern lies on the seam between strips 3 and 4 (figure 36).

This idea can be used in many variations (figure 37):
♦ the strips do not always have to be stitched in the same order;
♦ you can vary the width of the strips; the six strips added together, however, must add up to the same measurement as the radius of the circle, plus seam allowances (figures 38, 39).

Variation 4
You can experiment with strips of fabric the same thickness as the ring. Cut three strips from the full width of the fabric. Stitch these

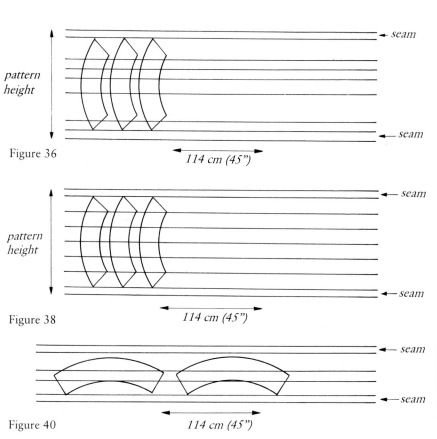

Figure 36

pattern height

114 cm (45")

Figure 38

pattern height

114 cm (45")

Figure 40

114 cm (45")

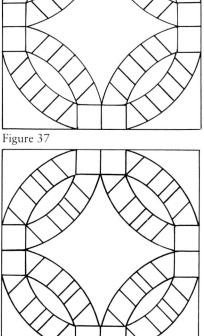

Figure 37

Figure 39

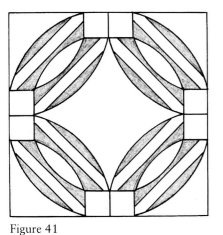

Figure 41

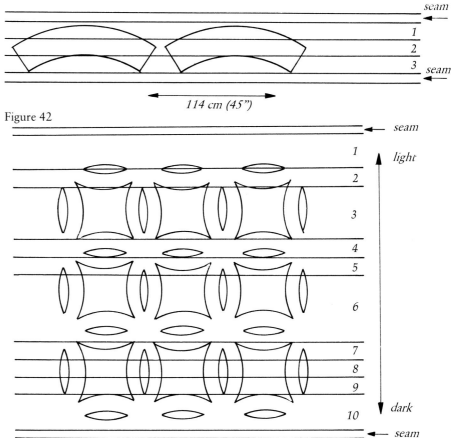

Figure 42

Figure 44

Figure 43

together and iron all the seams in one direction. Place the ring on the width of the new fabric (figures 40, 41).

Using this method more variations are possible:

♦ you could sew a number of smaller strips of fabric together;
♦ the strips of fabric need not all be the same size;
♦ one ring could be made from three and another from five strips;
♦ it is also possible to make variations inside the rings with horizontal or vertical strips (figure 43).

Variation 5
The rounded diamond and the moon shape together form the DWR.

By using different fabrics for the background many variations can be made on the traditional quilt.

Construct a piece of fabric of many different coloured strips to form a background for a Double Wedding Ring quilt. Make sure the piece of fabric is large enough. The strips can be the same size or different widths.

The colours should run from dark to light. Iron the piece flat and iron all the seams in the same direction.

Figure 45

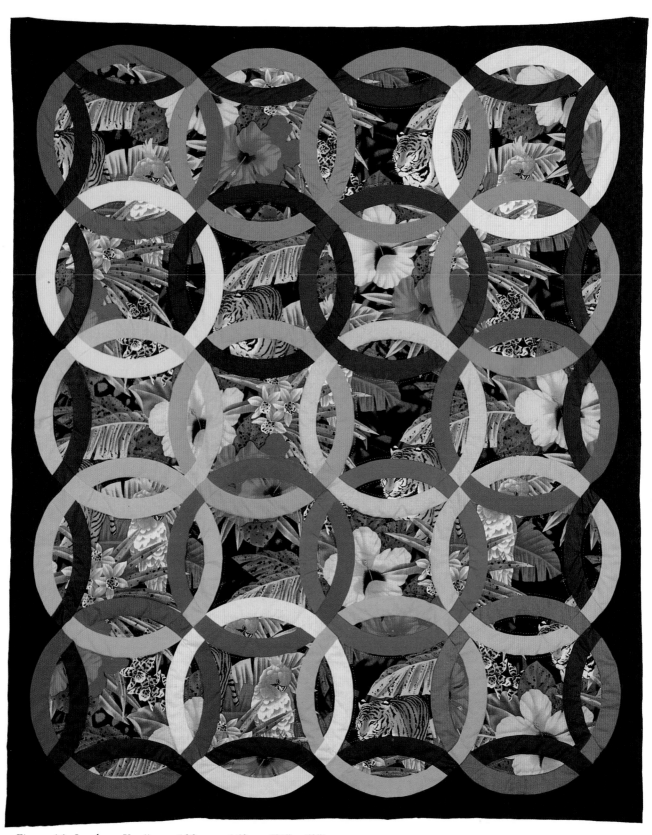

Figure 46 *Ingeborg Kooijman, 130 cm x 160 cm (51" x 63")*

Figures 47a, 47b *Variations on figure 47*

Figure 47 *Ingeborg Kooijman, 105 cm (41") square*

Position the patterns on the fabric in the right order (figures 44 and 45, page 13).

Variation 6
Using Crazy Patchwork make a piece of fabric the same size as the centre piece and position the patterns on it (figure 48).

Variation 7
The centre piece of the ring can be made as a block of patchwork or as appliqué.

For example, appliqué beautiful flowers on a light coloured background. You could also use other motifs such as cats or bears for appliqué. It is also possible to trace the shape of the hands of family, friends and relatives of the bridal couple and appliqué them to a background fabric. The handprints could even include the signature of each person. Be careful to keep the appliqués inside the circle.

Another possibility is to make the centre piece from patchwork. For example, you could make some small houses (figure 49). If a quilt like this was made for a golden wedding anniversary it could symbolise all the different houses the couple has lived in. For a married couple who love water sports, small boats could be made as the centre piece. Endless variations are possible, with stars, compasses, windmills, whatever.

Variation 8
Amish Nine-patch Wedding Ring: This pattern is made from squares, equilateral triangles and hexagons (figure 50). The sides of the square are the same length as the sides of the hexagon and triangle. In the example shown in figure 51 the side measures 9 cm (3⁹/₁₆").

The square of 9 cm x 9 cm is divided into nine squares, each measuring 3 cm x 3 cm (1³/₁₆" x 1³/₁₆").

To make a hexagon first draw a circle with radius equal to the length of the side of the hexagon, in this case 9 cm or 3⁹/₁₆" (figure 52).

Keep the compass at the same size (9 cm) and position the point at the top of the circle. Draw a curve to cut the circle. Position the compass point where the curve cuts the circle and draw another curve to cut the circle. Repeat this action five times (figure

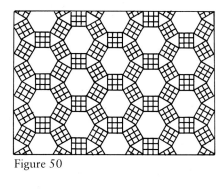

Figure 50

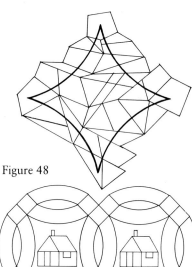

Figure 48

Figure 49

53). If this is done correctly the last point of intersection will be at the starting point. Join the points together to make a hexagon (figure 54).

An equilateral triangle can be made by drawing a hexagon and connecting all the points through the centre. A hexagon contains six equilateral triangles (figure 55).

Note: An easier way of making a triangle is to use isometric paper, which is divided into 60°.
Variations:
♦ divide the square into a different number of squares;
♦ divide the square into three equal strips (figure 56);
♦ make a combination of the three shapes.

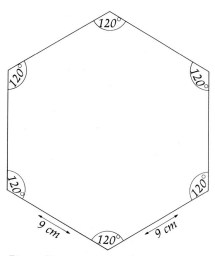

Figure 51

16

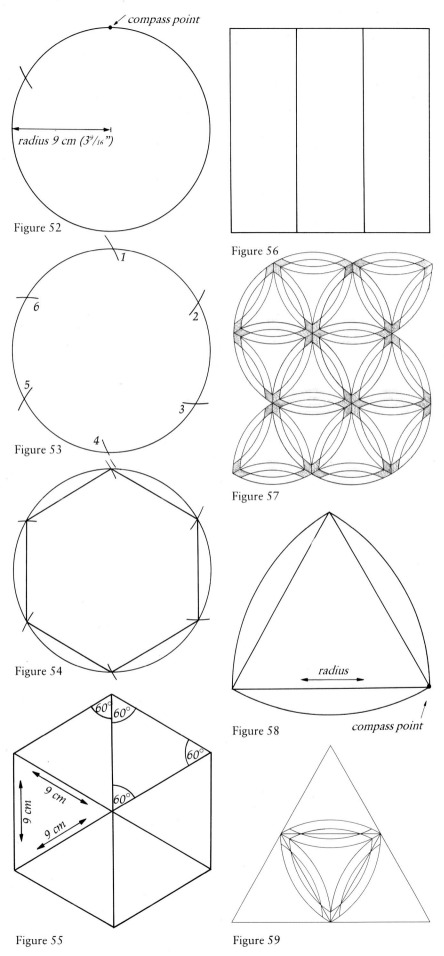

Figure 52

Figure 53

Figure 54

Figure 55

radius 9 cm (3⁹/₁₆")

compass point

Figure 56

Figure 57

Figure 58

compass point

radius

Figure 59

Variation 9

The basic shape of a normal Double Wedding Ring is a square. There are many other possibilities if the basic shape is changed, for example, the Diamond Wedding Ring (figure 57). This pattern is built up from equilateral triangles. You need isometric paper for this.

Set a radius on the compass equal to the length of the side of the equilateral triangle. Position the compass point in one corner and draw a curve from one opposite corner to the other opposite corner (figure 58). Do this from each point of the triangle. To draw the inside of the ring you will need to draw four triangles (figure 59). The radius for the inside of the rings is 8/9ths of the radius for the outside of the rings (figure 59). For example, if the outside radius was 9 cm (3½"), the inner radius will be 8 cm (3"). The points of the intersecting curves form a six-pointed star (figure 57).

Variations: Draw hexagons on isometric paper and use them as the basic forms for a Wedding Ring.

Making templates

The patterns for the templates must be drawn true to size. Before cutting out the pieces mark all the cutting points with matching pairs of symbols and number them individually (figure 62, page 20).

Draw a diagonal from top left to bottom right. The intersections of this line with the ring, the ellipse and the centre piece must be indicated on the drawing. The cutting points and crossing points will need to be marked on the fabric as well. Glue the completed drawing to a piece of medium thick cardboard or pattern board and cut the pieces out very carefully with a Stanley knife.

Templates for the sewing machine

If you intend to make the complete quilt on the sewing machine, it can be stitched on the pencil lines and the templates made to include a seam 7 mm (¹/₄") allowance. This is the distance from the needle to the outside of the foot of the sewing machine. (Check this measurement before making the templates, in case your machine is different.)

The templates are made in the same manner as those for hand sewing,

17

Figure 60   *Corrie Hagendijk, 200 cm x 260 cm (79" x 102")*

18

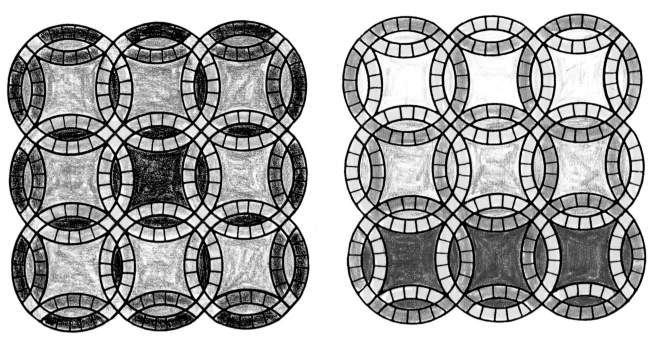

Figure 61a, 61b *Variations on figure 61*

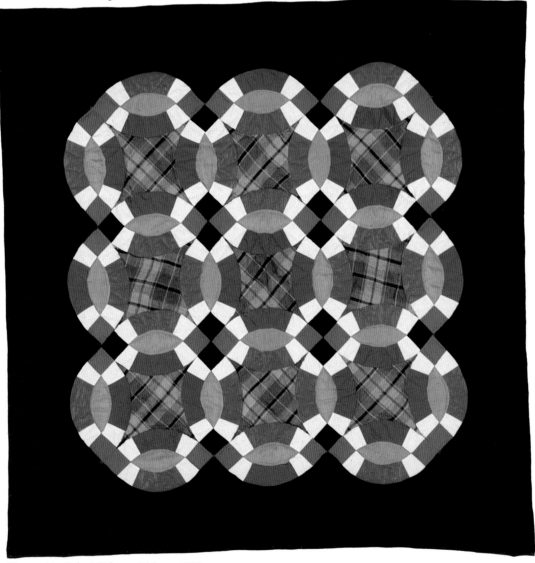

Figure 61 *Joke Nieboer, 132 cm (52") square*

19

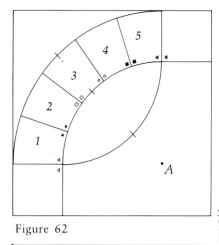

Figure 62

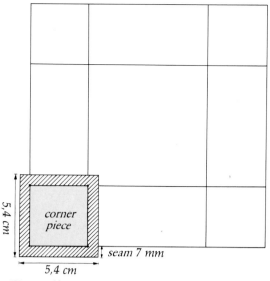

corner
piece

seam 7 mm

5,4 cm

5,4 cm

Figure 63

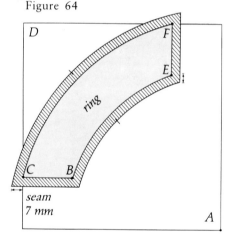

D   F

ellipse

B

E

C

seam
7 mm

A

Figure 64

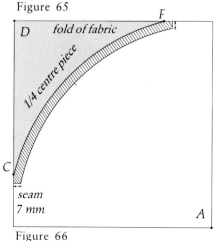

D   F

ring

F

E

C   B

seam
7 mm

A

Figure 65

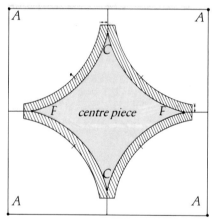

A   A

C

F   centre piece   F

C

A   A

Figure 67

D   fold of fabric   F

1/4 centre piece

C

seam
7 mm

A

Figure 66

adding an extra 7 mm (¹/₄") all the way around for seam allowance before cutting the pieces on the pencil line. The basic pattern pieces will all have to be drawn separately.

This example uses a round Double Wedding Ring.

The cornerpoint measures 4 cm x 4 cm (1¹/₄" x 1¹/₄"); adding a 7 mm (¹/₄") seam allowance makes the measurements now 5.4 cm x 5.4 cm (2¹/₈" x 2¹/₈") as shown in figure 63.

To make a seam allowance around the ellipse, first draw the ellipse without seam allowance. Place the point of the compass on point A and the pencil 7 mm (¹/₄") to the left of point B.

Draw a curve from B to E, extending it slightly past B and E (figure 64). Do the same from point D. Line up the ruler on the diagonal

from point A to D and mark the intersecting points on the ellipse (figure 64).

The inside of the ring is made by drawing a curve 7 mm (¹/₄") to the right of point B in line with A towards E (figure 65); the outside of the ring is drawn 7 mm (¹/₄") left of C in line with A to F (figure 65). Draw also a parallel line at a distance of 7 mm (¹/₄") from C to B and E to F. Place the ruler from A to D to draw in the crossing points (figure 65).

To make the centre piece: 7 mm (¹/₄") to the right of point C (from A) draw a curve in the direction of point F. This actually gives you only a quarter of the centre piece. The seam is added only to the rounded sides, not to the corner CDF, because CDF is placed on the fold of the fabric. Draw in the crossing lines (line AD, figure 66).

The centre piece should also be drawn true to size. Draw four connecting squares 16 cm x 16 cm (6" x 6"). Keep in mind that for a round Double Wedding Ring the circle point A is to the lower right. Continue in the same manner as before.

Remember to number the templates and indicate the crossing points described previously by the square Double Wedding Ring. It is important to mark the crossing lines of the stitching on the templates (B, C, E, F). Make a small hole in the template to be able to mark the fabric.

20

4 Assembling the Pattern

Cutting out the pieces

Cut out the templates and attach a piece of fine sandpaper to each corner, using small strips of 7 mm (¼") double-sided tape. Glue a sheet of fine sandpaper to a piece of timber the same size. This can be used as a base to prevent the fabric slipping.

Trace the templates with a pencil onto the reverse side of the fabric, marking in the cutting points and making sure the corners are very neat. Cut out the pieces with a 5 mm (³⁄₁₆") seam allowance for hand sewing.

If you are using a sewing machine your templates should have included a seam allowance of 7 mm (¼"). You can use a rotary cutter around the templates or trace the templates onto the fabric and cut around the pencil lines. Remember to mark the cutting points and crossing points on the fabric.

Sewing instructions

♦ When hand-sewing work from corner to corner, use two backstitches to start and the same for finishing. Between these points sew two running stitches and backstitch continually.
♦ Pin the pieces together very carefully.
♦ Make sure the crossing points fit together.
♦ Always place the pins *across* the pencil line, so that you can sew across the pins.
♦ Check to make sure the back seam stays on the pencil line.
♦ As far as possible when sewing, keep the hollow side of the curves up.

Order of sewing

♦ First sew the pieces together to form half a circle, making sure they are in the correct order (figure 68). Press the seams flat to one side.
♦ Sew the half circle to the ellipse.
♦ Pin the crossing points carefully together and press the seam towards the ellipse (figure 69).
♦ Sew another half circle and attach a corner piece at each end (figure 70).
♦ Attach this piece to the other side of the ellipse (figure 71).
♦ Always place the pins across the seams so that you can sew over them.
♦ In this manner make as many ellipses as required. Follow the diagrams to prevent mistakes.
♦ Sew four ellipses clockwise to the centre piece. Pin the pieces together, making sure the crossing points correspond, and sew the whole article from corner to corner with the hollow side uppermost (figure 74). The whole pattern is made entirely from these circles. Diagonally under each circle is a centre piece (figure 75).
♦ Sew the circles together in horizontal strips. Sew the centre pieces in between. Continue working strip by strip.

Instructions for sewing machine

♦ Use small stitches (1.5), to make stronger seams.
♦ Stitch everything from one outer edge to the other.
♦ It is not necessary to double-stitch at the beginning and end of each seam as the seams are strong enough without.
♦ The order in which the work is done by machine is the same as for hand-sewing.

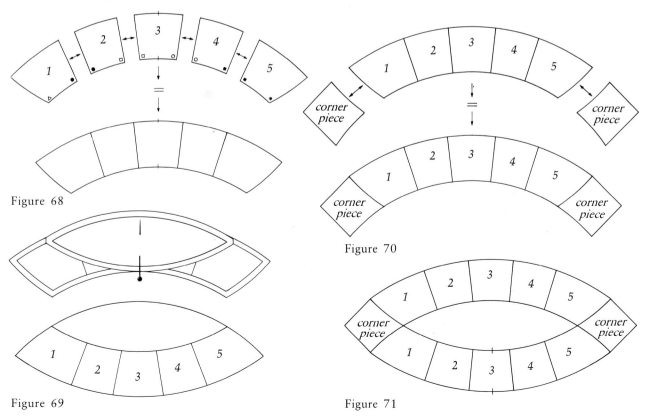

Figure 68

Figure 69

Figure 70

Figure 71

21

Figure 72 *Leny van der Werf, 97 cm x 115 cm (38" x 45")*

Figure 73a, 73b, 73c   *Variations on figure 73*

Figure 73   *Anja van Dommelen, 100 cm x 100 cm (39" x 39")*

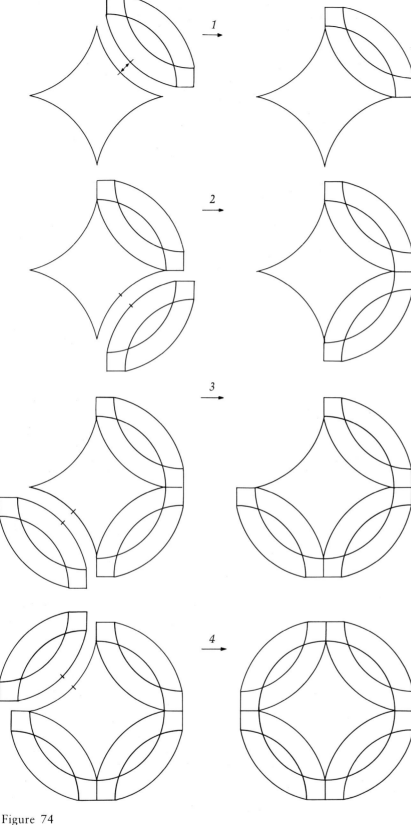

Figure 74

- ◆ Stitch the ellipses to the background fabric (figure 74). Do this from corner point to corner point, not from seam to seam. In this manner sew the rest of the quilt together.
- ◆ When sewing from corner point to corner point you will need to start as follows: sew a few stitches to the corner point, leave the needle in the corner, turn the work around and sew back to the other corner point. Leave the needle in the corner, turn the work around and finish off with a few stitches above the stitching line.

It is possible to finish off using the reverse sewing-machine foot method, although this can cause a thick knot underneath the work if the tension is not perfectly adjusted. The first method is a little more work, but the result is a lot neater.

Edges

You can make the Double Wedding Ring quilt with the arcs of the circles as the edge, like the yellow quilt made by Karin Jongeleen (page 30). The sculpted edge can be finished off with a bias binding, like the quilt made by Clara Janssens (page 11). A handmade border can also be very beautiful (pages 10, 14 and 15). The quality of commercial bias binding can be disappointing, because it has a tendency to fade rather quickly and can fray at the edges. If you intend to make your own edging you can do it with the same fabrics used in the quilt. During the quilting process the fibrefill or wadding (see following paragraph) sometimes shrinks a little, therefore it is advisable not to finish the edge or add bias binding until all the quilting has been done. A border along a Double Wedding Ring intended for a wall hanging will make it easier to hang while for a bed quilt the width of the border will depend on the size of the mattress. Stitch the border to the quilt before quilting the border.

Stretching

When the top of the quilt is finished to the required size, you will need to buy some fibrefill or wadding, available from most fabric shops or quilter's suppliers in different thicknesses and widths.

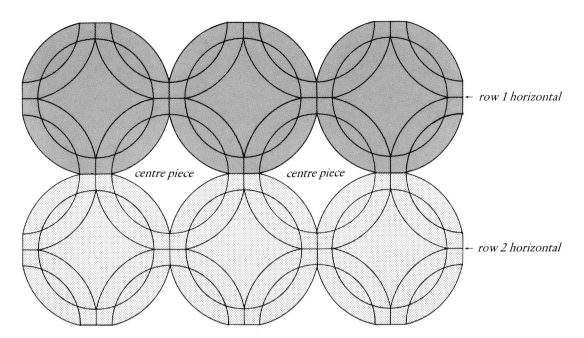

← row 1 horizontal

centre piece *centre piece*

← row 2 horizontal

Figure 75

Ideally the fibrefill should be a little wider than the quilt, but if the correct width is not available, it is a simple enough procedure to sew two widths of fibrefill together. To do this butt the two pieces against each other and sew them together with a fairly large overhand stitch. Small precise stitches are not necessary as the fibrefill will be held in place with all the quilting stitches. You could also use the zigzag stitch on the sewing machine.

Always cut the fibrefill larger than the size of the quilt, approximately 5 cm (2") all around. This is because the quilting can sometimes cause the fibrefill to shrink a little, so to be on the safe side always cut it a bit larger than the quilt.

The thickness of the fibrefill is dependent on the use intended for the quilt. If you are making a quilt for a wall hanging a thin fibrefill (40 g weight) would be sufficient. For a quilt to be used on a bed or sofa, you can choose from 40 g, 60 g or 80 g weights. The thicker the fibrefill the more difficult the quilting becomes and the more obvious is the quilted effect. Thick fibrefill will need more lines of quilting.

Keep in mind that fibrefill flattens with use. Cotton filling and cotton/fibrefill fillings are also available. Cotton filling is more difficult to quilt, but gives a beautiful heavy quilt.

For the backing you can choose a supple cotton fabric, which can

contain some synthetic. Wholly synthetic fabrics like artificial silk are not suitable for quilting because the needle tends to slip.

Your choice of backing fabric will depend on the article to be quilted. If you are making a wall hanging the backing fabric will not be visible. If the quilt is to be used on a bed the backing fabric will have a decorative function. The quilt can be used on both sides if the quilting work is very beautiful. If your quilt stitches are not very even and occasionally miss the backing fabric, it may be advisable to use a patterned backing fabric in the colour of the quilting cotton so that mistakes are not so visible. If, however, you are an experienced quilter a plain backing fabric will certainly show off your stitching to advantage. The backing fabric must be at least as large as the fibrefill and may or may not have seams in the length or width.

Before stretching the three layers, check the complete quilt top one more time. Check that the seams are all the same size. Cut away frayed and loose threads. Iron the reverse side, making sure the iron is not too hot. Synthetic sewing cottons and cotton fabrics that are not 100% cotton can melt. The seams are never ironed open but to one side. With see-through fabrics iron the seams to the darker side. After ironing the back, iron the front again to remove any

creases. Once the work is stretched it cannot be ironed any more.

Tape the backing fabric right side down with masking tape onto a solid background. Making sure the backing fabric is straight, place fibrefill on top. This does not need to be taped down.

Position the top of the quilt, right side facing, on top of the fibrefill. Check that the backing fabric and fibrefill are directly underneath and stick out a little on all sides. Tape the top down.

The three layers can be kept together in two different ways. The simplest way is to use safety pins, positioned at 15 cm (6") intervals through the three layers. This will require a large number of safety pins, no longer than 3 cm (1¼"). Never use this safety pin method with a silk quilt. Make sure the quilt is always stored in a dry place or the safety pins may rust.

The other method is to pin the three layers and then baste them together with a running stitch. Again the pins will need to be spaced at about 15 cm (6") intervals. The basting is done from the centre of the quilt in 15 cm (6") squares and the pins removed afterwards. Basting a big quilt is very labour-intensive work. As the quilting may take several months to complete it is very important that the three layers are kept together with very small stitches.

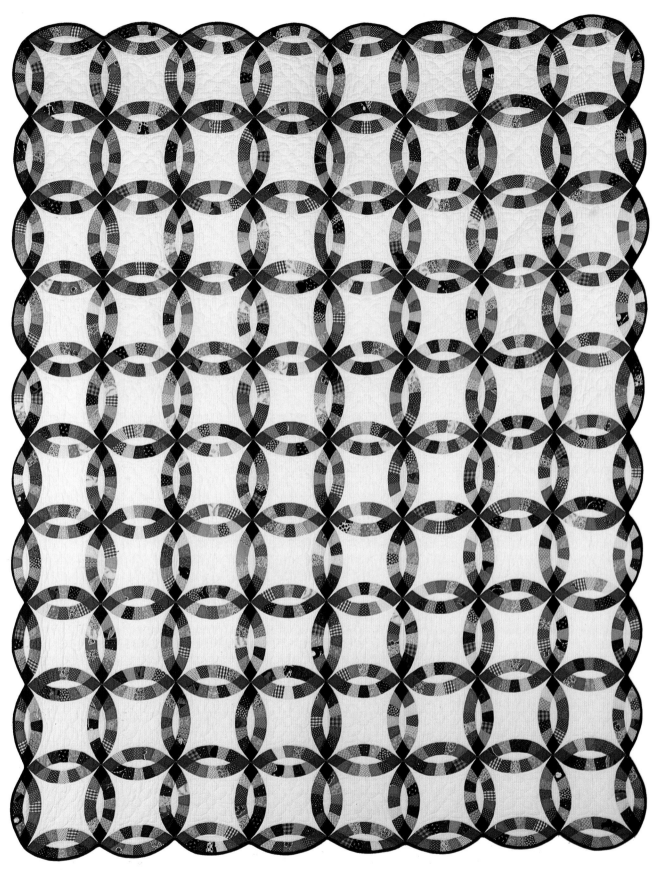

Figure 76   *Clara Janssens, 210 cm x 260 cm (82^1/$_2$" x 102")*

5 Quilting

Quilting is usually done with a quilting hoop and special quilting needles and cottons. The needles are small and strong. For beginners a no.8 (Milward) quilting needle is recommended. The larger the number the smaller the size of the needle and the more experienced the quilter needs to be. Quilting cotton has a special coating to protect the cotton against rough fibres in the fabric. Quilting cotton is usually 100% cotton, or cotton and polyester, and available in many colours.

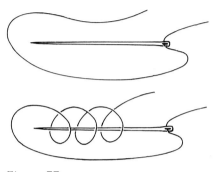

Figure 77

General recommendations
♦ Never use more than one colour for quilting a piece. If you are an experienced quilter you could choose a colour that contrasts with the work. If you are not quite so experienced it may be better to use a coloured cotton that blends in with the patchwork.
♦ Quilting is done at a distance of 5 mm (³/₁₆") from the seams.
♦ The quilt must be stitched evenly all over.
♦ Quilting stitches need to be small and very even.
  Quilting stitches are small running stitches that must be the same size at the front and the back of the work. This is not easy to do, but practice makes perfect.
  To start the quilting thread make a small knot in the end of the cotton and proceed as follows (figure 77).
♦ Place the end of the thread near the eye of the needle.

Figure 78

♦ Wind the thread three times around the needle.
♦ Pull these loops over the eye of the needle to the end of the thread.

Figure 79 *Detail of figure 76*

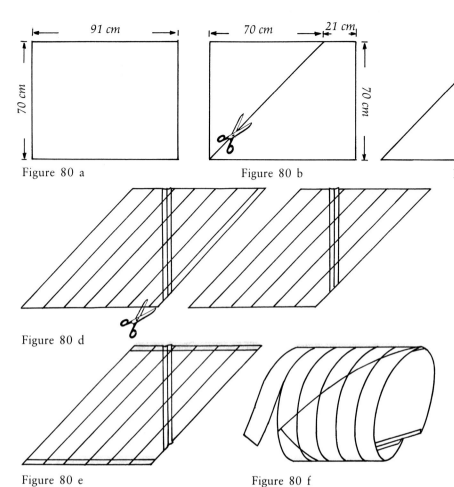

Figure 80 a

Figure 80 b

Figure 80 c

Figure 80 d

Figure 80 e

Figure 80 f

♦ Take the needle through all layers of the quilt and bring it out at the top of the quilt at the starting point.

♦ Pull the thread carefully through the fabric and the knot will disappear inside the fibrefill.

Make your quilting stitches very small and even. Take the needle straight down through the work and take it up again vertically. All the quilting is done with small, even-sized running stitches.

Use a small backstitch to finish off: that is, when you get to the last stitch, instead of going forward take the needle back through the last stitch. The needle will split the thread in two, holding it fast. Take the needle back through two layers, return to the top and cut the thread. Use a thread long enough to complete a section without starting a new thread in the middle.

The lines on the quilt can be marked with a special felt-tip marking pen. Two different sorts of pens are available. The water-erasable marking pen (purple in colour) makes a mark which is dissolved by the humidity in the atmosphere. This has the advantage that you do not need to wet the quilt to remove the marks. It is probably advisable not to make too many lines at the one time because on a really damp day the lines can disappear in twenty minutes. There is also a blue variant of this marking pen, erasable only with water. Always test these pens out on a small piece of waste fabric before using them, because they have been known to stain yellow fabric.

On dark fabrics you could use an aquarelle or a soap pencil.

You can use one of the many quilting patterns available in craft shops, or you could make your own. Cut a sheet of paper to fit the middle section of the ring pattern and fold it into eight (figure 78). Experiment with a pair of scissors and you could come up with your very own quilting patterns. You could also quilt a monogram in the centre of your quilt.

In the quilt by Leny van der Werf on page 22 large parts of the ring pattern are quilted instead of patched, while Joke Nieboer (page 19) has quilted the area around the rings in a triangle pattern. It is not essential to quilt each piece precisely 5 mm (³/₁₆") from the seams; you can use your imagination to create your own fantasies.

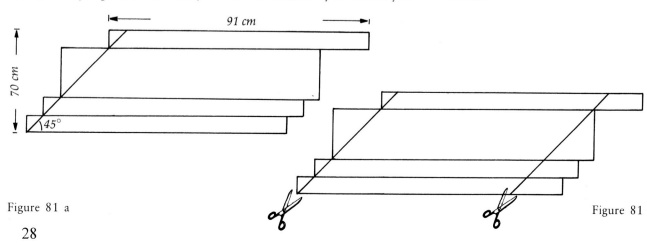

Figure 81 a

Figure 81

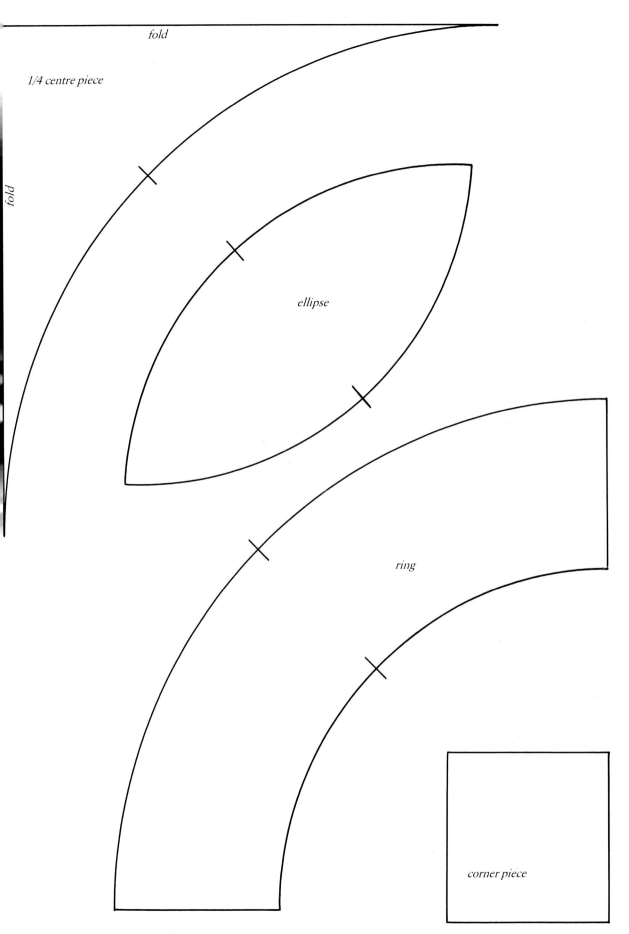

fold

1/4 centre piece

fold

ellipse

ring

corner piece

Figure 82 *Template for a square Double Wedding Ring*

29

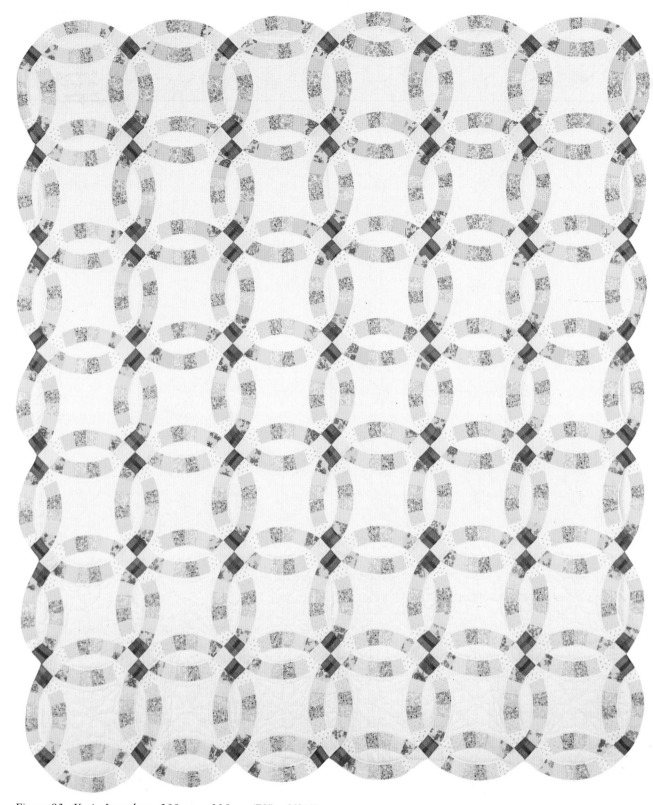

Figure 83 *Karin Jongeleen, 200 cm x 235 cm (79" x 92¹/₂")*

Finishing

Making borders
If you are going to make a border for your quilt, it can be as wide or narrow as you wish. In general a wide edging is more attractive. Double the fabric and stitch the border to the top of the three layers (top, fibrefill and back). You can use your own discretion as to how much of the border will be visible at the front.

The edging is attached by hand at the back of the work. As a general rule you will need a border approximately 6–8 cm. To work out how much fabric you will need if the perimeter of the quilt is 880 cm and the width of the edging is to be 7 cm, take the perimeter measurement and divide it by the width of the edging (880 ÷ 7 = 125).

As this is an approximation only it is better to estimate the perimeter at 910 cm, which is more evenly divided by 7 (910 ÷ 7 = 130). This calculation means you will need 9.10 m of 7 cm fabric. Moving the 0 from 910 from left to right tells you that a piece of fabric 91 cm x 70 cm will give 9.10 m of 7 cm edging.

Cut a rectangle of fabric measuring 91 cm x 70 cm (figure 80a).

At the left of the rectangle cut an equilateral triangle with its second side equal to the width of the rectangle, in this case 70 cm (figure 80b). Sew this triangle to the right hand side of the fabric to make a parallelogram (figure 80c).

On the back of the fabric draw lines the width of the edging running parallel to the bias of the fabric. The strips must all be the same width. Any left over strips not the right size should be discarded (figure 80d).

Draw a line 1 cm from the edge at the top and bottom. These are the stitching lines for joining the pieces of the edge (figure 80e).

Fold the fabric inside out, so that all the lines are visible. Make sure all the lines continue on. Leave a piece at the top as well as the bottom. This will give a spiral effect (figure 80f). On the 1 cm line stitch the spiral together and cut the lines that were drawn from top to bottom.

Follow the same procedure for a quilt made in Imperial measurements.

The edging can also be made in several colours, a process which is simpler than it looks. An interesting finishing touch is to use all the colours of the quilt in the edging.

Make a parallelogram in a variety of colours. The strips will all need to be the same length (in our example 91 cm); the widths can vary.

Stitch the strips together. Make sure you have a 45° angle (figure 81a). When the piece is the required size—in our example 70 cm—cut a right and a left corner of 45° off (figure 81b).

This will give a piece as shown in figure 80c. Continue working in the same manner following figures 80a to f. This method will use more fabric, so keep this in mind.

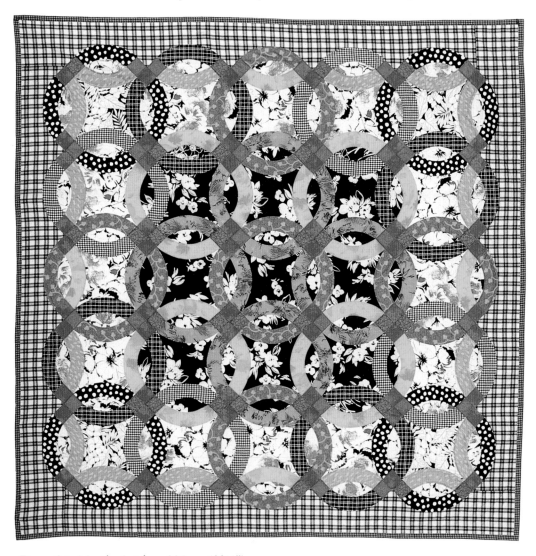

Figure 84 *Marijke Snijders, 225 cm (88½") square*

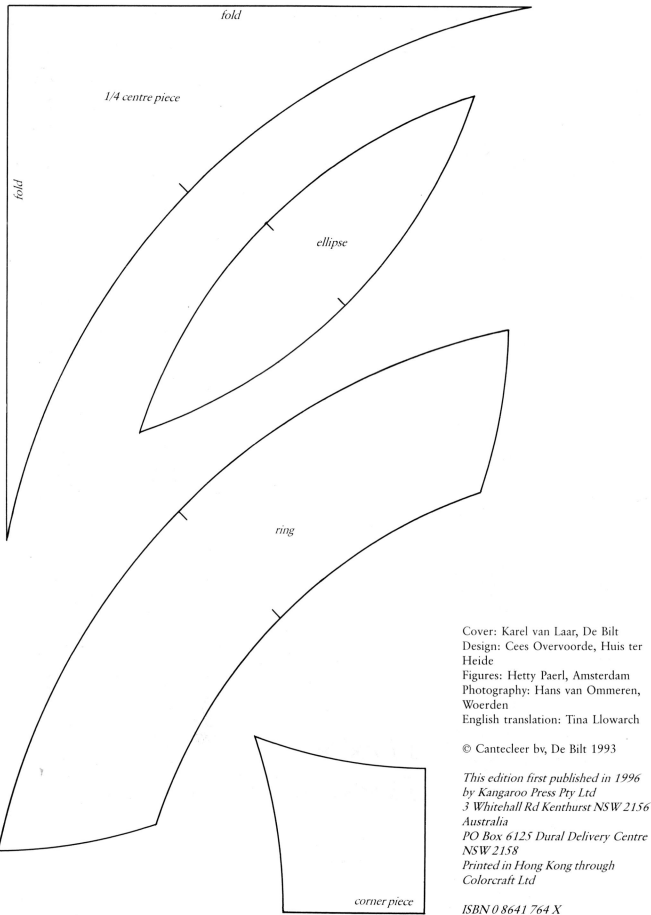

fold

1/4 centre piece

fold

ellipse

ring

corner piece

Cover: Karel van Laar, De Bilt
Design: Cees Overvoorde, Huis ter Heide
Figures: Hetty Paerl, Amsterdam
Photography: Hans van Ommeren, Woerden
English translation: Tina Llowarch

© Cantecleer bv, De Bilt 1993

This edition first published in 1996 by Kangaroo Press Pty Ltd 3 Whitehall Rd Kenthurst NSW 2156 Australia PO Box 6125 Dural Delivery Centre NSW 2158 Printed in Hong Kong through Colorcraft Ltd

ISBN 0 8641 764 X

Figure 85 *Templates for a round Double Wedding Ring*